PERSUASION

by Jane Austen

Adapted by Jeff James, with James Yeatman

ıl SAMUEL FRENCH lı

samuelfrench.co.uk

FOR AMATEUR PRODUCTION ENQUIRIES

UNITED KINGDOM AND WORLD
EXCLUDING NORTH AMERICA
plays@samuelfrench.co.uk
020 7255 4302/01

Each title is subject to availability from Samuel French,
depending upon country of performance.

THINKING ABOUT PERFORMING A SHOW?

There are thousands of plays and musicals available to perform from Samuel French right now, and applying for a licence is easier and more affordable than you might think

From classic plays to brand new musicals, from monologues to epic dramas, there are shows for everyone.

Plays and musicals are protected by copyright law so if you want to perform them, the first thing you'll need is a licence. This simple process helps support the playwright by ensuring they get paid for their work, and means that you'll have the documents you need to stage the show in public.

Not all our shows are available to perform all the time, so it's important to check and apply for a licence before you start rehearsals or commit to doing the show.

LEARN MORE & FIND THOUSANDS OF SHOWS

Browse our full range of plays and musicals and find out more about how to license a show

www.samuelfrench.co.uk/perform

Talk to the friendly experts in our Licensing team for advice on choosing a show, and help with licensing

plays@samuelfrench.co.uk   020 7387 9373

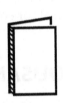
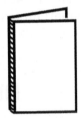

MUSIC USE NOTE

Licensees are solely responsible for obtaining formal written permission from copyright owners to use copyrighted music in the performance of this play and are strongly cautioned to do so. If no such permission is obtained by the licensee, then the licensee must use only original music that the licensee owns and controls. Licensees are solely responsible and liable for all music clearances and shall indemnify the copyright owners of the play(s) and their licensing agent, Samuel French, against any costs, expenses, losses and liabilities arising from the use of music by licensees. Please contact the appropriate music licensing authority in your territory for the rights to any incidental music.

USE OF COPYRIGHT MUSIC

A licence issued by Samuel French Ltd to perform this play does not include permission to use the incidental music specified in this copy. Where the place of performance is already licensed by the PERFORMING RIGHT SOCIETY (PRS) a return of the music used must be made to them. If the place of performance is not so licensed then application should be made to the PRS, 2 Pancras Square, London, N1C 4AG (www.mcps-prs-alliance.co.uk).

A separate and additional licence from PHONOGRAPHIC PERFORMANCE LTD, 1 Upper James Street, London W1F 9DE (www.ppluk.com) is needed whenever commercial recordings are used.

JEFF JAMES

Jeff James' work as a director includes *La Musica* at the Young Vic; *Stink Foot* at The Yard, which he adapted from Sophocles' *Philoctetes*; *One For the Road* and *Victoria Station* at the Young Vic and Print Room.

JAMES YEATMAN

As writer/director: *Still Ill, Dog Show* (New Diorama) *Limehouse Nights* (Limehouse Town Hall)
Director: *Radio* (Soho Studio/59e59 Theatres New York)

James is an associate artist with Complicite for whom he was the co-adapter/director on *The Kid Stays In The Picture* (Royal Court) and *Beware of Pity* (Schaubuhne), the co-director on *Lionboy* (Tricycle and international) and the associate director on *The Master and Margarita* (Barbican and European Tour).

AUTHOR'S NOTE

Some people don't like Jane Austen. They might worry that Austen believed that marriage was the only thing that made a woman's life meaningful. Some of her characters do believe this some of the time, but the idea is interrogated and discredited in all of her novels.

Jane Austen's central question is how you should organise your life – how to balance competing demands like sex, money and family. It's obvious that we still grapple with these tensions today: we're still trying to find good ways of living with a partner or on our own, good ways of dealing with our parents, of finding a home, of having children or not having children.

Austen wouldn't recognise many of the ways we live now, but the intelligence with which she analyses these choices felt strikingly contemporary to me when I first read *Persuasion*. Austen insists that the choices in our private lives are important: not only is it possible to ruin your life if you choose poorly, but these choices are fundamental in shaping your character and identity.

Persuasion is a rom-com: there is a pleasure in following Anne and Wentworth's misadventures, wondering if they will find a way back to each other. But there's a deeper pleasure as Austen uses courtship and romance to examine integrity and selfhood. Anne learns the hard way that our deepest feelings are to be trusted, and that ignoring one's desires creates contradictions that are ultimately unsustainable. The joy of the novel is that Anne is given a second chance to choose what kind of life she wants.

Jeff James
May 2017

First commissioned by and received its world premiere at Royal Exchange Theatre, Manchester, on 1 June 2017, with previews from 25 May 2017. The cast was as follows:

LADY RUSSELL/MRS CROFT	Geraldine Alexander
SIR WALTER/ADMIRAL CROFT	Antony Bunsee
MARY	Helen Cripps
CAPTAIN WENTWORTH	Samuel Edward-Cook
ELIZABETH/LOUISA	Cassie Layton
MRS CLAY/HENRIETTA	Caroline Moroney
ANNE	Lara Rossi
CHARLES	Dorian Simpson
EDMUND/CAPTAIN BENWICK/MR ELLIOT	Arthur Wilson

Director – Jeff James
Designer – Alex Lowde
Lighting Design – Lucy Carter
Music and Sound Design – Ben and Max Ringham
Movement – Morgann Runacre-Temple
Dramaturg – James Yeatman
Assistant Director – Helen Abbott

CHARACTERS

ANNE
MRS CLAY / HENRIETTA
SIR WALTER / ADMIRAL CROFT
ELIZABETH / LOUISA
LADY RUSSELL / MRS CROFT
MARY
CHARLES
WENTWORTH
EDMUND HAYTER / CAPTAIN BENWICK / MR ELLIOT
SAMUEL, a little boy

Part One: Kellynch
Part Two: Uppercross
Part Three: Lyme Regis
Part Four: Bath

For Joan and Frank James, and Colin and Betty Jacobs.
True models of constancy.

"Well life has some risks. Love is one. Terrible risks."
Anne Carson, *The Beauty of the Husband*

With thanks to these readers of early drafts for their
generosity and intelligence: Suzanne Bell, Amy Clewes,
Tracey Elliston, Matthew Evans, Sarah Frankcom,
Joe Hill-Gibbins, Lillith Glimcher, Phoebe James,
David Lan, Rachel Lincoln and Nina Segal.

This script went to press during rehearsals, and may differ
from the text in performance.

PART ONE: KELLYNCH

1

ANNE is lying face down on the floor, as if she has fallen out of the sky. As the other characters play the scene around her she slowly comes to. ANNE is always on stage. Everything happens to her.

Enter SIR WALTER *and* MRS CLAY.

SIR WALTER If one visits her in daylight, she lowers the blind. One sits in darkness. A lady of that age suffers dreadfully, of course. One pities her.

MRS CLAY Lady Russell should use more rouge. I do not know how I would live without it.

SIR WALTER You are kind to Lady Russell, but this is far too modest. A young lady needs no artificial aid to her radiance.

MRS CLAY You flatter me, Sir Walter. I am a widow, not a young girl.

SIR WALTER Nature alone flatters you, Mrs Clay. You are a very pretty, very young widow. Time will see you courting again soon. What can cosmetics do for youthful perfection?

MRS CLAY Sir Walter!

SIR WALTER Although you're never too young to start using Gowland's. I do recommend the daily application of Gowland's lotion, expensive though it is. You would be surprised to learn, I think, that Lady Russell and I are almost of an age.

MRS CLAY Sir Walter, that cannot be possible.

SIR WALTER Gowland's.

Enter **ELIZABETH.**

ELIZABETH Father, I have had a letter from Mr Assingham.

MRS CLAY Finally!

SIR WALTER Is he coming to visit?

ELIZABETH Mr Assingham is not going to visit Kellynch Hall. The letter does not even mention his promise of a visit. All the promises he made in London are forgotten, or ignored.

SIR WALTER How could he have forgotten you?

MRS CLAY What is the subject of his letter?

ELIZABETH It is an invitation. An invitation to the wedding of Mr Frank Assingham and Miss Lucy Pulford.

MRS CLAY Oh, Elizabeth, I'm so sorry.

SIR WALTER But he seemed madly in love with you.

MRS CLAY Who is Lucy Pulford?

ELIZABETH She is the daughter of Sir Edward Pulford. His eighteen-year-old daughter.

SIR WALTER Oh God. I was sure he would propose. This is a blow.

MRS CLAY Yes, but it is one we shall overcome. Countless eligible men would seek the hand of Elizabeth Elliot of Kellynch Hall.

ELIZABETH Where are they, Penelope? Father is the only man I have seen in the past six weeks. Mr Assingham is hardly the first gentleman to disappoint me in this way. There have been twenty. Thirty! You remember Mr Elliot?

SIR WALTER I do not wish to discuss that gentleman.

MRS CLAY Who is Mr Elliot?

ELIZABETH Our cousin. And Father's heir presumptive.

SIR WALTER He hasn't spoken to us in ten years. Mr Elliot has shown no respect to me.

ELIZABETH Mr Elliot courted me for months and months, and then he met some horribly vulgar woman and married her instead.

MRS CLAY Wouldn't that have been a bit peculiar though, to marry your cousin?

ELIZABETH Not in the slightest. What do you mean by that, Penelope? It would be a very proper match. Without a son, Father's estate will pass entire to Mr Elliot. Had he married me, Kellynch Hall would have remained in our part of the family.

SIR WALTER This is all best forgotten, Elizabeth.

ELIZABETH No Father – Mr Elliot's wife is now dead. Mr Elliot has become a widower and I am still a maid. An old maid.

SIR WALTER You are not old, Elizabeth. You are as blooming as ever. Think of your sisters. Anne is quite haggard at twenty-seven. Even Mary is grown coarse.

ELIZABETH No doubt Mr Elliot will be engaged to some girl of eighteen before the year is out.

MRS CLAY It is a shame that we cannot spend more time in London.

ELIZABETH Father, Penelope is quite right: we must go to London.

SIR WALTER We will be there in the winter.

ELIZABETH By the time winter comes, I will be thirty. I am approaching the years of danger, and every week my hopes narrow. London is full of eligible men who would be glad to make my acquaintance.

SIR WALTER It is too great an expense to stay in London for months on end.

ELIZABETH Such an expense should be nothing to the master of Kellynch Hall. We will go to London next week and remain there until the end of the season.

SIR WALTER Elizabeth, it is impossible.

ELIZABETH Nonsense!

SIR WALTER Our situation is far more precarious than you imagine. We cannot afford it. Every day another tradesman leaves a bill. We must find a way to retrench.

ELIZABETH We have already made economies.

SIR WALTER And we fall still further into debt. We will be ruined if we continue in this way.

ELIZABETH I must be married, Father, and there are no men here.

SIR WALTER I will consult Lady Russell: she will find a clever way for us to recover our position.

2

Enter **LADY RUSSELL.**

LADY RUSSELL These debts must be paid, Sir Walter. A simpler way of living will release you from financial embarrassment.

SIR WALTER Elizabeth has gone over the accounts and can find nothing. We live a very simple life.

ELIZABETH We have cut off all unnecessary charities.

SIR WALTER We didn't bring any presents back from London for you, or for Anne.

ELIZABETH I thought we could delay new-furnishing the drawing room.

SIR WALTER That's a capital idea. Well done Elizabeth.

ELIZABETH The essential object is that we spend more time in London: at present we are there for only a few weeks of the season. That is no time to meet anyone at all.

LADY RUSSELL Any stay in London is out of the question until you have found economies at home. Anne and I have marked out a scheme of retrenchment.

ELIZABETH Anne?

SIR WALTER Anne?

ELIZABETH What do you have to do with this? You know nothing of the accounts.

LADY RUSSELL Anne has looked into it closely and has many excellent proposals. If you adopt these regulations, in seven years you will be clear.

SIR WALTER We will have to retrench for seven years?

LADY RUSSELL Yes, unless you can find even greater economies.

ELIZABETH We can't wait seven years to return to London.

SIR WALTER I had thought it would take a few months.

ELIZABETH In seven years I will be thirty-six years of age.

LADY RUSSELL Sir Walter, these debts must be cleared with all possible speed or you will be ruined. That is your choice and to my mind it is an easy one.

SIR WALTER Tell me what we must do.

LADY RUSSELL Anne, would you like to begin?

ANNE *does not speak.*

A great deal could be saved by reducing the staff of Kellynch Hall.

SIR WALTER Right. We could probably manage with fourteen, or even twelve.

LADY RUSSELL We would reduce them to six.

ELIZABETH Kellynch Hall is far too large to have only six servants.

LADY RUSSELL Six would be plenty if you were to close the north wing and live only in the main part of the house.

ELIZABETH The north wing is my favourite wing.

SIR WALTER Do you have other proposals?

LADY RUSSELL You cannot hope to keep more than two horses.

SIR WALTER With two I would be unable to run the carriage.

LADY RUSSELL We propose you sell the carriage.

ELIZABETH Lady Russell, our dignity will not survive such measures. Anne is welcome to spend her time reading books and pottering about in the garden. Father is the master of Kellynch Hall, he is obliged to live in a certain style.

SIR WALTER I would rather quit Kellynch Hall than remain in it on such disgraceful terms.

LADY RUSSELL What did you say Sir Walter?

SIR WALTER I said I would rather quit Kellynch Hall.

LADY RUSSELL I did not have the wit to consider it, but that may be where your salvation lies.

ANNE Lady Russell?

SIR WALTER Where?

LADY RUSSELL In leaving Kellynch Hall.

ANNE Lady Russell?

LADY RUSSELL You could establish yourselves very happily in a smaller property, without the gross expenditure of running this house.

ELIZABETH You can't ask Father to live in a cottage in the village.

LADY RUSSELL It needn't be in this neighbourhood. You could move to town and enjoy a far wider society.

ANNE I want to stay here!

ELIZABETH Do you mean that we could live in London?

ANNE London is far too expensive for Father.

LADY RUSSELL Not London, but it would be possible for you to live at Bath.

ELIZABETH Bath?

ANNE Bath?

SIR WALTER I do like Bath.

LADY RUSSELL In Bath, your father will be important even after the necessary reduction in his means.

SIR WALTER The society in Bath is very fine. Beautiful women. Very fine eligible men.

ANNE Lady Russell!

LADY RUSSELL The concerts and dances are equal to anything in London. I am certain that both Elizabeth and Anne will enjoy themselves there.

ANNE I don't like Bath!

MRS CLAY I like Bath. There are such fine gentlemen there. If you can't find a husband in Bath, you won't find one anywhere.

    ANNE *gets rid of* **MRS CLAY.**

ANNE And what will happen to Kellynch Hall?

LADY RUSSELL We would find a tenant. They would pay rent and that would allow you to live comfortably in Bath.

ANNE I don't want to go to Bath.

SIR WALTER There will be many exceptional applicants who would pay handsomely to rent Kellynch Hall.

    ANNE *gets rid of* **SIR WALTER.**

ELIZABETH I will need some new dresses as soon as we get to Bath.

    ANNE *gets rid of* **ELIZABETH.**

3

ANNE Bath? You want us to move to Bath?

LADY RUSSELL I'm sorry Anne.

ANNE We never talked about Bath.

LADY RUSSELL It became clear that there was no other way for your father to lessen his expenses.

ANNE Bath is a very unpleasant town. It is busy and noisy and dirty.

LADY RUSSELL Your mother loved Bath.

ANNE Kellynch Hall is my home – I want to stay here.

LADY RUSSELL You can't live with your father's tenants.

ANNE But I could stay with you.

LADY RUSSELL I won't be here. I am spending the rest of the year in Yorkshire.

ANNE I could come with you to Yorkshire.

LADY RUSSELL Anne. You can't live with me forever.

Enter **ELIZABETH**.

ELIZABETH Anne, have you been using Father's Gowland's lotion?

ANNE No, I haven't seen it.

ELIZABETH He is grown quite distracted. We cannot leave without it.

ANNE It must be in his dressing room.

ELIZABETH No, I've looked there.

ELIZABETH *exits.*

LADY RUSSELL You'd rather stay here?

ANNE If they all go to Bath, Kellynch Hall will be a paradise.

LADY RUSSELL *(as SIR WALTER)* My Gowland's, my Gowland's. Elizabeth, I cannot for the life of me put my hand on my Gowland's lotion.

ANNE *(as ELIZABETH)* Father, when did you see it last?

LADY RUSSELL *(as SIR WALTER)* I had it in my hand but three minutes ago. All I have done in the interim is pull out the grey hairs from my nose.

ANNE *(as ELIZABETH)* But there is another one grown there already.

LADY RUSSELL *(as SIR WALTER)* Oh how the years betray me!

ANNE *(as ELIZABETH)* Even Mrs Clay won't love you now!

LADY RUSSELL *(as SIR WALTER)* O time! O mortality!

ANNE *(as ELIZABETH)* I must be married, Father! I want to go to all the dances and have all the fashionable dresses and meet every man in the world just in case one of them will be foolish enough to marry me.

LADY RUSSELL *(as herself)* Elizabeth is right that she should be more in society. The same is true for you.

You need to be more in the world Anne. You are twenty-seven years old. It is high time that both you and Elizabeth were married. Bath has many diversions for a clever and beautiful young woman. You will soon forget Kellynch Hall. Just don't forget me.

ANNE How could I?

LADY RUSSELL I will expect you to teach me all the new dances when I join you in the spring.

ANNE Goodbye, Lady Russell.

LADY RUSSELL Try and enjoy yourself.

Exit LADY RUSSELL.

4

Enter ELIZABETH.

ELIZABETH Anne, have you finished packing?

ANNE I have some small errands to run first. It won't take me long to pack.

ELIZABETH What errands? We must leave for Bath this afternoon.

ANNE I thought I would visit the different houses in the parish to say goodbye. If we are to be away from Kellynch for a year or more, I would not have them think us careless of our duty.

ELIZABETH This is overly-dutiful.

ANNE I must also set out which of your flowers are to be taken by Lady Russell and which to remain. I will also pay a visit to Mary: she wrote this morning and is not in good health.

ELIZABETH Mary is always ill. If you visit her this afternoon, she will demand that you stay there until Christmas. We need to leave.

ANNE We may not see her for many months. I think we could at least visit our sister on the way.

ELIZABETH I don't want to visit Mary. I don't want to visit every parishioner in Kellynch. I don't want to rearrange the garden. Any delay in our arrival at Bath may lose me the chance of a husband.

Enter SIR WALTER *and* MRS CLAY.

SIR WALTER The carriage is loaded up.

ELIZABETH Anne is not at all ready. She would have us call at Mary's.

ANNE Mary is not well.

SIR WALTER If we call on every sick acquaintance between Kellynch and Bath, we will never arrive.

ANNE Mary is your daughter.

ELIZABETH If you want to see Mary, it is no concern of mine. But you will have to find your own way to Bath. We cannot delay.

ANNE Perhaps I could stay at Uppercross until the spring and then travel to Bath with Lady Russell when Mary is better.

ELIZABETH It is entirely as you wish. Penelope will be with me. You are not needed in Bath, Anne.

ANNE Father, would you object to my staying at Uppercross?

SIR WALTER Why should I object? I suppose Mary may object.

ELIZABETH Mary has asked for Anne.

SIR WALTER Then it is settled: Anne should go where she is wanted.

ANNE I'm certain that Mary will be glad to have me with her.

SIR WALTER You will be only three miles from Kellynch – you will enjoy the society of our new tenants.

ANNE You have found someone to rent the house?

MRS CLAY Yes! An admiral!

ANNE An admiral?

SIR WALTER It will sound good to tell people "I have let my house to admiral" whoever it is.

Much better than saying "I have let my house to Mr –" whatever it may be. A Mr always needs a note of explanation.

ELIZABETH Who is this admiral?

MRS CLAY Admiral Croft.

ANNE Admiral Croft.

MRS CLAY He is a married man, but without children.

ANNE Yes.

SIR WALTER The name of Kellynch Hall was very well known to Mrs Croft. Her brother lived near here some years ago. I've forgotten the name of the brother.

ANNE Eight years ago.

MRS CLAY Exactly. The brother is much younger, but also naval, a captain.

SIR WALTER What was his name?

ELIZABETH Oh you mean Captain Wentworth?

SIR WALTER That's right. Captain Wentworth.

MRS CLAY Yes Captain Wentworth.

> ANNE *gets rid of* MRS CLAY.

SIR WALTER Oh yes. Frederick Wentworth!

> ANNE *gets rid of* SIR WALTER.

ELIZABETH Didn't you know him, Anne? Captain Frederick Wentworth.

> ANNE *gets rid of* ELIZABETH.

PART TWO: UPPERCROSS

5

There is a lot of mess. **SAMUEL,** *a little boy, is running around and playing.*

MARY Anne, you're much earlier than you said you'd be. I haven't even started cleaning the house.

ANNE Mary, it's fine.

MARY I've been on my own since seven o'clock this morning. I can barely stand. I can't eat anything. My head hurts. I can hardly speak. Samuel! Samuel! SAMUEL! Come here. Say "Hello Auntie Anne".

SAMUEL Hello Auntie Anne.

He immediately runs off again.

ANNE Hello Samuel. Where's Charles?

MARY He went shooting first thing. Charles expects me to look after Samuel and tidy the house even though my head is ringing with pain. He doesn't care at all.

ANNE Of course he cares.

MARY Where is he then? He'll do anything to get out of the house. He just wants to get away from me.

ANNE Perhaps we should go out too.

MARY We can't go to the big house.

ANNE Why not?

MARY Charles's sisters have to call on you here before we call on them. You are my guest and they should think what is due to you as my sister.

ANNE Mary, how can Henrietta and Louisa visit me when they don't even know that I'm here?

MARY Charles's family know everything else that happens in my house, I shouldn't expect your arrival has escaped their attention. No detail is too small for their criticism. I don't know why I ever agreed to live a quarter of a mile away from my in-laws.

ANNE *gets rid of* MARY.

Enter CHARLES.

CHARLES Hello Anne!

ANNE Hello Charles.

CHARLES How are you? I was so sorry to hear about Kellynch Hall. I know how you love that house.

ANNE There was nothing else to be done. I'm glad to have a reason to visit you and Mary here.

Enter MARY.

MARY Where have you been?

CHARLES I told you I was going shooting.

MARY Yes and you said you wouldn't be long.

CHARLES I lost track of time.

MARY You're lucky I'm not dead on the floor.

CHARLES You should get out of the house. Why don't you go and see my sisters?

MARY What is wrong with you both? They have to call on Anne first.

ANNE I would never think of standing on such ceremony with
the Musgroves.

CHARLES It doesn't matter, Mary.

MARY Of course it matters. Your family ignore every aspect of
decorum. Do you realise that last night I was served fourth
at supper?

CHARLES It's their house, Mary. You can't make everyone follow
your rules.

MARY They're not my rules, it's decorum. It's what everyone
does except your family.

CHARLES It's not what everyone does. Half of it's invented by
your father.

MARY Oh. I see. You're going to insult my father in front of Anne.

ANNE Don't be silly Mary.

MARY All I want is for people to behave with respect when
they are in my house.

CHARLES Everyone respects you, Mary.

MARY I haven't forgotten your mother leaving the room before
I'd even stood up.

CHARLES She didn't mean any harm Mary.

MARY In my house she should follow my rules.

CHARLES In a way it's her house.

MARY What do you mean by that?

CHARLES Nothing.

MARY No, what do you mean by that? "It's her house".

CHARLES All I mean is that, as a matter of fact, my parents
very generously gave us this cottage to live in.

MARY Where else were we going to live?

CHARLES You might just remember, as a matter of observable fact, that they gave us the cottage and helped pay for its improvement.

MARY Oh thank you for reminding me, yet again, of the debt we owe to your parents.

CHARLES I just think you could show some gratitude.

ANNE *gets rid of* CHARLES.

MARY I think they could show some respect.

ANNE *gets rid of* MARY.

6

Enter **LOUISA** *and* **HENRIETTA.**

HENRIETTA and **LOUISA** Anne!

LOUISA How lovely to see you Anne!

HENRIETTA We're so excited to have you with us.

LOUISA It is so kind of you to come and see us instead of going straight to Bath.

HENRIETTA You're such a good person.

LOUISA Are you going to live in Rivers Street?

HENRIETTA Or in Gay Street?

LOUISA Or Camden Place?

ANNE I don't know.

HENRIETTA Laura Place is the very best address. You don't want to be in Queen's Square.

LOUISA We will be there before the end of the season.

HENRIETTA We love it there.

Enter **MARY.**

MARY You've only been there once.

LOUISA And we loved it.

HENRIETTA The people of Bath are unbelievably sophisticated.

LOUISA Every new dance is invented in Bath.

HENRIETTA You must ask Elizabeth to send us each dance she learns.

LOUISA Anne, would you like to learn our new dance?

MARY Anne doesn't want to dance.

LOUISA She may do. Would you like to dance, Anne?

ANNE I'm a little tired from my journey. Why don't you two show me?

LOUISA Mary, count time.

MARY Is it a three one or a four one?

HENRIETTA It's an eight one.

MARY One two three four five six seven eight. One two three four five six seven eight.

> **MARY** *continues to count in a not very engaged way as* **HENRIETTA** *and* **LOUISA** *practise.*

HENRIETTA Will you be the man, Louisa?

LOUISA No, you be the man, Henrietta.

HENRIETTA But I'm always the man.

LOUISA When we get to Bath there will be real men to dance with.

HENRIETTA What do you mean?

LOUISA Well, who is there around here except Edmund?

ANNE Who's Edmund?

LOUISA Henrietta's admirer.

MARY He lives at Winthrop. It's a small house a mile or so away.

LOUISA Mary you mustn't just stop counting.

HENRIETTA It's not such a small house, and besides Edmund is the oldest son. And he is training to become a vicar.

ANNE I'll count time. One two three four five six seven eight.

LOUISA In Bath, there will hundreds of oldest sons to choose from. You don't want to get stuck dancing with just one man.

HENRIETTA The problem is that if you get asked to dance you have to say yes.

LOUISA That's not true, Henrietta. You may simply say that you are tired and will not dance again that evening.

HENRIETTA Yes, but then you have to stop dancing. Don't you see? What if you admire one gentleman, but someone else asks you to dance first?

LOUISA Then you must say yes to the first gentleman. Anne, I did not know that you had such a gift for the piano.

HENRIETTA But what if you don't want to dance with him? It would be much easier if a woman could ask a man to dance.

LOUISA Don't be absurd, Henrietta. That would be like a lady proposing marriage to a gentleman.

They both find this idea hilarious.

ANNE Do you have an admirer, Louisa?

ANNE *continues to count. She's better at it than* MARY.

HENRIETTA Louisa is so particular.

LOUISA Don't go so far away.

HENRIETTA No one is right for her.

LOUISA That's not true Henrietta.

HENRIETTA You'd better be careful or you'll end up an old maid.

MARY Henrietta!

LOUISA Henrietta, that's not a kind thing to say.

HENRIETTA Oh, I'm sorry Anne – I didn't mean to upset you.

ANNE ...One two three four five six seven eight. I do not mind Hen – ri – et – ta. One two three four five six seven eight.

ANNE *counts faster and faster. She finds a way to get rid of* HENRIETTA.

LOUISA Anne could easily find a husband, Henrietta. Twenty-seven is hardly a great age. Not every man is looking only for youth and beauty.

ANNE *gets rid of* LOUISA.

7

Enter **ADMIRAL CROFT, MRS CROFT** *and* **CHARLES.**
SAMUEL *starts making a lot of noise.*

MRS CROFT We were pleased to meet your sisters, Charles.

ADMIRAL CROFT They are delightful girls.

MRS CROFT Henrietta showed us her beautiful drawings.

ADMIRAL CROFT Which one was Henrietta?

MRS CROFT The one who had made the drawings. The one who is to marry the vicar.

MARY Oh, we do not think she will marry him. It is a youthful fancy that will pass.

CHARLES Nonsense, Mary.

MARY Samuel! Samuel be quiet! I'm so sorry.

ADMIRAL CROFT It is a novelty for us. We are quite charmed by young Samuel.

CHARLES He has been shut up in the house all day. No wonder he is irritable.

MARY How can I watch him in the garden when I have so much to do in the house?

MRS CROFT Frederick will be very glad to meet both your sisters, I am sure.

MARY Frederick?

MRS CROFT My brother. Captain Frederick Wentworth. He has just been paid off and will be living with us at Kellynch.

ADMIRAL CROFT Kellynch Hall is far too big for just us two.

MRS CROFT You must still consider it your home, Miss Anne. Call on us there whenever you care to.

ANNE You're very kind, but Mary needs my help here.

MARY No I don't.

MRS CROFT Well you must come next week.

ANNE When will your brother join you at Kellynch?

> **SAMUEL** *is still kicking off – maybe throwing stuff at the adults.*

CHARLES Mary, just take him outside.

MARY Is Captain Wentworth a single man?

MRS CROFT Yes. Frederick has been married to the sea these past eight years.

ADMIRAL CROFT I'm sure he would be glad to meet Louisa now he is on shore.

MARY And Henrietta.

CHARLES Edmund Hayter would have something to say about that.

MARY Henrietta Musgrove of Uppercross would do better to think of naval heroes than country vicars.

ANNE Henrietta is very fond of Edmund. I think it is a sincere attachment.

MARY What does that have to do with anything?

MRS CROFT Miss Anne does well to look beyond Mr Hayter's fortune. Romance must have its share as well as prudence.

MARY You misunderstand me, Mrs Croft. Edmund Hayter has no fortune whatsoever.

MRS CROFT When I married the admiral he had scarcely a penny to his name.

ADMIRAL CROFT Well, Frederick will be here tomorrow. We should let the young people meet before we determine their futures.

MARY I'm sure that your brother will enjoy Henrietta's drawing as much as you did, Mrs Croft.

CHARLES He must come for dinner tomorrow night. We'd all love to meet him.

ANNE *gets rid of* **CHARLES**.

MRS CROFT I'm surprised that he is unknown to you. Frederick lived in this part of the world in the year six.

MARY I would have been away at school then. Anne would have been at Kellynch, though.

ANNE *gets rid of* **MARY**.

ADMIRAL CROFT Anne did you ever meet Frederick?

ANNE *gets rid of* **ADMIRAL CROFT**. *She turns around and* **MRS CROFT** *is* **LADY RUSSELL**, *in 1806*.

ANNE Lady Russell?

LADY RUSSELL Anne, listen to what I am saying. I cannot bear to see Anne Elliot throw herself away at nineteen to a man with no fortune – with no real prospects. Prudence must have its share, as well as romance. If you marry Captain Wentworth, your future would depend on his success in a most uncertain profession. By twenty-five you would be a mother, a widow even: your father would not be able to support you.

I can't stop you Anne, but I know what your mother would say if she were alive now. It is senseless to rush into this attachment. You are so young. You have so much time, Anne.

8

Enter **HENRIETTA** *and* **LOUISA**.

HENRIETTA I cannot wait to meet Captain Wentworth.

LOUISA They say he made a great fortune in the war.

HENRIETTA I'm certain that he will be a fine dancer.

LOUISA I like the Crofts very much – Mrs Croft's brother is sure to be an extraordinary gentleman.

HENRIETTA The Crofts are very different to how I imagined naval people to be.

LOUISA What do you mean Henrietta?

HENRIETTA I thought they would find it peculiar to be back on land, having been so many years at sea. I was surprised that they enjoyed mutton, and didn't ask for fish instead.

LOUISA Come on, we're going to be late. People eat mutton at sea Henrietta.

HENRIETTA It will be such a fine party at the big house. Anne, after supper you can play the piano.

ANNE I am feeling a little unwell. I might prefer to stay at the cottage this evening.

MARY Nonsense, Anne. It will do you good to be in new company.

HENRIETTA I hope Captain Wentworth will ask me to dance.

SAMUEL *starts chanting* "**CAPTAIN WENTWORTH**".

LOUISA You don't want to make Edmund jealous.

HENRIETTA Edmund has no right to be jealous. It is not as if we are engaged. Anne, what music will you play?

ANNE I think it would be better if Mary played for you this evening. I am very tired and ought to stay here.

LOUISA Anne, you must come. Mary is so much less delicate in her playing than you.

HENRIETTA How your little fingers fly about!

LOUISA I dance far better when you are playing, Anne.

ANNE I am not well.

MARY You can't stay here, Anne – we would be an odd number at supper.

HENRIETTA You were feeling fine earlier.

LOUISA My parents would think it very odd if you did not come now.

   ANNE *gets rid of* SAMUEL.

SAMUEL Mummmmmmmyyy!!!

   SAMUEL *falls to the ground.*

9

MARY Samuel! Oh my God my child my child. Charles! He's going to die he's going to die he's going to die. Charles!

HENRIETTA Anne – what should we do?

Enter **CHARLES.**

CHARLES What's happened?

LOUISA Samuel has fallen from a tree.

CHARLES My God.

ANNE He's hurt his shoulder.

MARY Is it broken? Has he hit his head?

HENRIETTA and LOUISA Poor little Samuel.

ANNE I think it's alright. He's just bruised. I don't think it's broken.

MARY What shall we do? What shall we do?

ANNE There's not much we can do.

LOUISA Poor Samuel.

CHARLES Well this rather scuppers our dinner with the Crofts.

HENRIETTA But Captain Wentworth is coming.

LOUISA We were going to dance with Captain Wentworth.

HENRIETTA If we must stay with Samuel, perhaps we could invite Captain Wentworth here.

ANNE You should both go without us. We do not all need to attend to Samuel.

HENRIETTA Who will play the piano?

ANNE I'm sorry. Please send our regards to the Crofts.

LOUISA Of course. I hope Samuel's alright.

HENRIETTA Bye-bye little Samuel!

Exit HENRIETTA *and* LOUISA.

CHARLES It is a great shame that we won't have the chance to meet Captain Wentworth. He sounds like a most interesting gentleman. He's been all over the world. The West Indies, the East Indies, the Western Isles, the Eastern Isles.

MARY If you'd been watching Samuel instead of thinking about Captain Wentworth, he wouldn't have hurt himself. Then we would be having supper with Captain Wentworth now.

CHARLES Mary –

MARY I'm playing with Samuel.

CHARLES I bet they're having a great time over there. How's Samuel getting along, Anne?

ANNE He's improving a little.

CHARLES If he carries on like this, I could join them at the big house later.

MARY What do you mean?

CHARLES I wouldn't have dinner there, but I could walk in for half an hour or so and meet this Wentworth.

MARY And what would Captain Wentworth think of a father who goes out to a party when his son and heir is dying?

CHARLES He's not dying Mary. If he is to be kept in bed and quietly amused, what is there for a father to do? This is quite a female case and it would be ridiculous for me...

MARY A female case? What do you mean by that – a female case?

ANNE Charles is right, Mary. We can manage here. You should go over to the big house, Charles.

CHARLES *exits.*

MARY So you and I are to be left by ourselves with this poor sick child. Men find a way out of anything disagreeable. That's what you learn when you're married Anne. They're never there when you need them. Charles actually doesn't care. He doesn't care about his own son. He only cares about meeting Captain Wentworth.

ANNE Mary, I can look after Samuel on my own. Why don't you join Charles and go to the big house?

MARY That's a very good idea, Anne. I love my son as much as any mother, but I can't bear to see Samuel like this. You're right, I should go. Captain Wentworth would think it rude if I wasn't there.

MARY *goes*.

10

WENTWORTH *enters.*

WENTWORTH Excuse me, madam.

ANNE Oh.

WENTWORTH I was hoping to find your brother-in-law at home.

ANNE I haven't seen him yet this morning.

WENTWORTH He invited me to go shooting. I had thought you were with your family in Bath.

ANNE No, I'm staying with my sister. With Mary and Charles.

WENTWORTH I'm staying with my sister. She and the admiral are now living at Kellynch Hall, as you must know.

ANNE Yes.

WENTWORTH I'll see if Charles is outside.

MARY *enters.*

MARY Oh, you found your way here, Captain Wentworth? We had such a wonderful time last night Anne. Captain Wentworth said that he knew you when he was here in 1806.

ANNE We were acquainted.

MARY We had so much more fun than we normally do at the big house. The admiral and Mrs Croft are such kind people, Captain Wentworth, and so polite.

WENTWORTH The admiral and my sister are honoured to be such welcome guests at Uppercross.

MARY I had always thought of sailors as quite rough people, but in fact you're all twice as civilised as my husband's family.

WENTWORTH I hope your son has recovered from yesterday's fall.

MARY Oh, I think he's fine.

CHARLES *enters.*

CHARLES Mary, have you seen my gloves?

MARY No of course I haven't.

CHARLES Good morning Wentworth.

WENTWORTH Good morning.

CHARLES We picked a fine day for it. We'll have some good sport this morning.

WENTWORTH I hope so.

CHARLES I'm sure they were in this jacket. You must have taken them. Wentworth, have you been introduced? This is Mary's sister, Anne. Anne, this is Captain Wentworth. They're not in this jacket.

MARY They're your gloves Charles, not mine.

WENTWORTH We are acquainted.

CHARLES Oh of course, you said last night. I'm sure they were in here. Wentworth, I'll meet you outside.

CHARLES *and* MARY *exit.*

WENTWORTH Good morning to you madam.

ANNE Good morning to you sir.

WENTWORTH *exits.*

11

LOUISA *and* HENRIETTA *enter.*

LOUISA You missed a splendid evening, Anne.

HENRIETTA I have never met a gentleman like Captain Wentworth.

LOUISA You've never met a naval gentleman before, Henrietta.

HENRIETTA The Navy has done so much for our country. I truly believe it is our greatest institution.

LOUISA What about the Church, Henrietta?

HENRIETTA I say nothing against the Church, I'm only praising the Navy.

LOUISA Well don't let Edmund hear you say that. He will think you prefer Captain Wentworth.

Enter **MARY.**

MARY Captain Wentworth is not very gallant by you, Anne. He told Charles that he would not recognise you had he not known you were my sister: he found you so changed from when he knew you in the year six.

13

Enter **CHARLES.**

CHARLES Wentworth is an incredible shot. You will have your chance with him this evening, Anne: he is dining at the big house again. Let's hope that Samuel doesn't have any more accidents.

14

LOUISA, HENRIETTA, WENTWORTH, ANNE, CHARLES, MARY, ADMIRAL CROFT *and* **MRS CROFT** *are at dinner.*

LOUISA Captain Wentworth, tell Anne what you told us last night about the Asp.

HENRIETTA Tell us about the Navy and about your ships and how you made your fortune.

LOUISA It is not fair that Anne's dutiful attendance on Samuel should deprive her of such entertainment.

WENTWORTH Whatever meagre enjoyment it might offer Miss Elliot, I would certainly bore all of you who indulged me yesterday.

HENRIETTA No, I long to hear it again.

WENTWORTH I will serve you in any way at my disposal, except in this instance.

LOUISA If you will not tell the story, then I will. Anne. Captain Wentworth left England in 1805.

WENTWORTH 1806!

LOUISA 1806. He was first made captain of the Asp, a worn-out old sloop. The Navy had declared her unsafe to leave the channel, but Captain Wentworth took her to the West Indies, to the Western Isles, to Gibraltar and back to Bermuda.

HENRIETTA Aren't the Western Isles and the West Indies the same isles?

LOUISA No they are not Henrietta.

ADMIRAL CROFT That is an error in navigation that could put you out by some three thousand miles, Miss Musgrove.

LOUISA Anne, can you credit his bravery? The Asp was a ship in which few would dare to cross the Irish Sea – but Captain Wentworth circumnavigated the globe in her!

WENTWORTH I did no such thing!

CHARLES I still cannot understand how the Navy would allow you to go across the Atlantic in such a worn-out old thing.

WENTWORTH For their amusement. In this case, they never had the pleasure of reading that I had been sent to the bottom.

ADMIRAL CROFT What stuff these young fellows talk. Believe me, Anne, there were twenty men who would have given their eye-teeth to take the Asp.

WENTWORTH I felt my luck, believe me admiral.

LOUISA To conclude this story, Anne: Captain Wentworth had nothing when he was made captain of the Asp – within two years he had found fame and fortune.

MRS CROFT Louisa, you exaggerate. His success was no great surprise. Even when Frederick was a lieutenant, we all knew he was one of the Navy's brightest men.

WENTWORTH This is nothing more than a sister's partiality.

MRS CROFT Anne you knew Frederick before he took his commission, in 1806?

ANNE Yes.

MRS CROFT And was it easy to see the success he would have?

ANNE I think...

WENTWORTH You must not interrogate Miss Elliot, Sophy.

LOUISA I'm sure he was every inch the hero we see today.

WENTWORTH I was a boy. I knew nothing of the world.

ANNE I remember that Captain Wentworth was determined to get to sea.

LOUISA Determined to save the nation from France.

WENTWORTH I wanted to be doing something.

LOUISA Such modesty!

WENTWORTH There was nothing for me in England.

ADMIRAL CROFT What should a young single fellow do ashore for half a year together? Now you have a decent fortune, you'll find yourself a wife.

WENTWORTH I fear few women could enjoy the manners I've cultivated in eight years at sea.

MRS CROFT Frederick, you are too subtle. Last night he told me he would take any pretty and lively woman between fifteen and thirty.

WENTWORTH Sophy!

LOUISA If you are to find a wife then you must dance, Captain Wentworth. Will you dance now?

WENTWORTH I fear you will find me very deficient. I am much out of practice.

LOUISA Then you must get into practice.

HENRIETTA We will be gentle with you.

WENTWORTH I will submit to your tuition.

ADMIRAL CROFT Will you dance, Anne?

ANNE No. Thank you admiral, but I must play the piano.

ADMIRAL CROFT Will you partner me, Mrs Croft?

MRS CROFT With pleasure, admiral.

MARY You could ask me to dance, Charles.

CHARLES Alright, Mary. Would you like to dance?

MARY Yes I would thank you.

Everyone dances except **ANNE.**

15

CHARLES I have never met a more pleasant man in my life.

MARY He must have made twenty thousand pounds in the war. That is a fortune at once.

CHARLES And think what he might make in the next war.

MARY Captain Wentworth seems highly likely to distinguish himself.

CHARLES He would be a good match for either of my sisters.

MARY It would be a great thing for Henrietta, don't you think Anne?

CHARLES Or for Louisa.

MARY He much prefers Henrietta.

CHARLES If Henrietta marries Edmund, and Louisa has Captain Wentworth I shall be very pleased.

MARY Captain Wentworth might be made a baronet. Henrietta could become Lady Wentworth. That would sound good.

CHARLES Louisa could just as happily be Lady Wentworth.

MARY He clearly likes Henrietta a good deal the best.

CHARLES Anne, who do you think Captain Wentworth prefers?

MARY You must agree that he is wholly for Henrietta.

CHARLES Nonsense, he much prefers Louisa. Here's Edmund anyway.

EDMUND HAYTER *enters.* **HENRIETTA** *is in* **WENTWORTH***'s arms.*

HENRIETTA Edmund!

EDMUND Henrietta.

HENRIETTA Edmund!

> **EDMUND** *runs off.* **HENRIETTA** *tries to follow him but he gets away. Everyone gives up on dancing.*

16

ANNE *is left on stage. Alone, she dances.* SAMUEL *enters and starts to annoy her. He manages to find a way to climb up on her back and she can't get him off.*

ANNE Samuel, get down from there. Samuel. Samuel, get down this moment. You are extremely troublesome. I am very angry with you.

WENTWORTH *enters and manages to remove the boy quickly and deftly.*

WENTWORTH Samuel has evidently recovered from his fall.

ANNE At his age, they cannot be laid low for very much time at all.

WENTWORTH I have observed that a shock which would put me out of action for weeks is felt as nothing by a little boy. Or a little girl.

ANNE It may be that each subsequent shock teaches the body what it means to fall.

WENTWORTH *(to* SAMUEL*)* You are a brave and good little boy. But you must not bother your aunt so. She has many important occupations. Do you understand, Samuel?

SAMUEL Yes, Captain Wentworth.

ANNE Were you hoping to find the Miss Musgroves here, Captain Wentworth?

WENTWORTH Indeed I was, although I see no sign of them.

ANNE They are at the big house.

WENTWORTH Then I will search for them there. Good afternoon, Miss Elliot.

17

HENRIETTA Edmund has invited me to go to Winthrop this evening.

ANNE That's nice, Henrietta.

HENRIETTA I am not at all sure that I will go.

ANNE Why wouldn't you go?

HENRIETTA He behaved so foolishly the other evening, storming off as soon as he saw me dancing with Captain Wentworth. I think he might call on us again here before expecting me at Winthrop.

ANNE If you would like to see Edmund, I think you should go.

HENRIETTA Captain Wentworth is coming here tonight. I'd much rather stay here and see him.

ANNE Then you ought to stay here.

HENRIETTA But I wouldn't want to upset Edmund.

ANNE Henrietta, you need to decide what you want. Last month you seemed very keen on Edmund.

HENRIETTA We've been having so much fun now you're here, and Captain Wentworth.

ANNE Do you love Edmund?

HENRIETTA I don't know.

ANNE Or perhaps you love Captain Wentworth.

HENRIETTA Anne! I hardly know him.

ANNE Well, quite.

HENRIETTA Edmund would make a very good husband. He's kind, and dependable, and honest. But his prospects are very uncertain. He will have very little money before he inherits. We may have to live with his parents for years. Mary thinks that I could find a far better husband.

ANNE Other people will try to persuade you of a thousand different things. You must listen to your heart. I had – I had a friend who had a similar choice to make. She loved a man whose fortune was uncertain, far more uncertain than Edmund's. When he proposed, her family, without absolutely forbidding the match, advised her to refuse him. They believed she could find a far better husband.

HENRIETTA And did her family succeed in persuading her?

ANNE They did. She declined the proposal and broke off from him.

HENRIETTA And did she marry someone better?

ANNE There was no one better. Whatever his circumstances, her first love was her only love. A few years later, another man proposed. He could have offered her a comfortable, secure existence. She couldn't say yes to him, knowing that she loved another. She never married.

HENRIETTA She was foolish not to take the second gentleman's offer. This is what I am afraid of. Edmund is far from perfect, but imagine being left on my own. The trouble is it's impossible to know what will happen in the future.

ANNE What will you do this evening?

HENRIETTA I don't know. What do you think I should do?

ANNE I think you should decide. You can't have dinner here and at Winthrop.

HENRIETTA Very well. I will go to Winthrop. It would be unkind to deny Edmund an opportunity to apologise. Louisa can entertain Captain Wentworth.

18

LOUISA and WENTWORTH *meet and sit together.* ANNE *can hear them but they don't know that.*

WENTWORTH Are we alone, Miss Musgrove? I had expected to find your brother.

LOUISA Charles is shooting.

WENTWORTH And Mrs Musgrove?

LOUISA Mary is sick.

WENTWORTH But Henrietta will be joining us?

LOUISA Henrietta? No. She has gone to Winthrop. She will be there all evening.

WENTWORTH I see.

LOUISA She has decided to forgive Edmund.

WENTWORTH The circumstances of their quarrel are rather obscure to me.

LOUISA Henrietta simply could not decide what she wanted. She appeared determined to marry him but Mary had convinced her that she could find a far better husband.

WENTWORTH Henrietta would do well to look into her heart.

LOUISA Mary should leave her alone. She is such a meddler. I wish Charles had married Anne instead.

WENTWORTH Anne?

LOUISA Yes.

WENTWORTH There was a question of that?

LOUISA Of course. He asked Anne first.

WENTWORTH Do you mean that she refused him?

LOUISA Oh yes.

WENTWORTH When was this?

LOUISA I do not know exactly. While I was at school. I told Henrietta she must be firm. It doesn't matter what Mary thinks of Edmund: it is Henrietta who is going to marry him.

WENTWORTH Henrietta is fortunate to have a mind such as yours to advise her.

LOUISA When I am determined on a course of action, Captain Wentworth, nothing may divert me. I am not easily persuaded.

WENTWORTH If Louisa Musgrove is to be as beautiful and happy in her November of life, she should remain firm. That is my first wish for all whom I love.

LOUISA All whom you love?

LOUISA *kisses* WENTWORTH.

WENTWORTH To my mind, the worst fault of character is to be yielding and indecisive: you cannot trust such a person, anybody may sway them. Let she who would be happy be firm and seize hold of what she wants, even as the whole world warns her that she may not have it. How can you love someone who's shifting, who's inconstant?

LOUISA You cannot. You must not.

WENTWORTH I have a friend, a brother officer, who was engaged to be married. They had had to wait a year or so for fortune and promotion. She was a wonderful woman, Felicity Harville, and my friend Benwick's love for her was pure and true and good. Fortune came, promotion came, but Felicity did not live to see it. Benwick is a serious, thoughtful man, and is terribly affected by the change. I would see him happy again, but I know that his affection is Felicity's, even now she is dead. He is a true model of constancy. He lives alone now at Lyme Regis, mourning his loss.

LOUISA At Lyme Regis?

WENTWORTH Yes.

LOUISA Oh Captain Wentworth, couldn't we go and visit the poor man? I have heard so much of the beauty of the coast at Lyme.

WENTWORTH I did have an idea of visiting him.

LOUISA I am sure that Captain Benwick would welcome the distraction of your company. And I would love to go to the sea with you.

WENTWORTH Perhaps Anne could come too. And Henrietta. And Mary and Charles.

MARY Where are you going?

LOUISA We're going to Lyme Regis.

MARY It's seventeen miles away.

HENRIETTA What's happening?

LOUISA We're going to Lyme Regis. Bring Edmund.

HENRIETTA I can't. He has to study.

LOUISA Whoah! We're going to Lyme Regis!

Whoah! Back to the island!

Whoah! We're going to have a party!

Whoah! In the Mediterranean sea!

PART THREE: LYME REGIS

19

WENTWORTH, LOUISA, ANNE, HENRIETTA, CHARLES *and* **MARY** *stare out to sea.*

LOUISA Look, Captain Wentworth, it's the sea.

WENTWORTH "All must linger and gaze on a first return to the sea, who ever deserve to look on it at all".

LOUISA Where's that from?

ANNE I've never seen the sea. It's beautiful.

Enter **BENWICK**.

BENWICK Wentworth!

WENTWORTH Benwick!

WENTWORTH *and* **BENWICK** *hug. Proper love.*

Benwick, let me introduce you: Charles and Mary Musgrove. Charles's sisters, Louisa and Henrietta Musgrove. And this is Miss Anne Elliot. Captain Benwick is the finest lieutenant I ever met, an excellent cook and an appalling snorer.

BENWICK I am more or less the only lieutenant he ever met. Wherever Wentworth was posted, he was saddled with me as his junior.

WENTWORTH All the education a life at sea could afford me I owe to Benwick. New books were all that he thought of, whenever we found ourselves ashore. How do you like Lyme?

BENWICK   It provides what I need. There is peace here. I read. I watch the sea. I think about the past.

HENRIETTA   Have you been to Lyme Regis before, Captain Wentworth?

WENTWORTH   Once. Two years ago, Benwick and I had a week on shore and came here with...

BENWICK   We were on holiday here with Felicity Harville. Perhaps Wentworth has told you something of this.

WENTWORTH   Something of it.

BENWICK   You didn't come to Lyme to hear about my sadness.

LOUISA   Frederick, let's go down to the beach. I'll race you.

WENTWORTH   What? Alright.

> **WENTWORTH** *hares after* **LOUISA; HENRIETTA, CHARLES** *and* **MARY** *follow;* **ANNE** *is left with* **BENWICK.**

20

BENWICK Wentworth is in high spirits today.

ANNE He has deserved a holiday, has he not, Captain Benwick? Peace has been hard won.

BENWICK At sea, Wentworth had a keenness of intellect and a strength of nerve that made him a model for all.

ANNE There must have been occasional moments of levity, even aboard a ship.

BENWICK Of course, but we never encountered anyone quite like Louisa Musgrove during the Napoleonic wars.

ANNE Perhaps nothing in peace-time will show Captain Wentworth's full potential.

BENWICK Let Wentworth have his fun. When wars end, men turn to courtship. The peace won't last forever.

ANNE I'd rather have a war than another conversation about who someone's going to marry.

BENWICK The choice will determine the rest of their lives, it is an important question.

ANNE But it is not the only question. I feel as if the world looks at a woman closely for six months as she chooses between one, or two or perhaps three suitors. Once she has chosen, the reader is no longer interested and the book is closed. Her story ends with her wedding, and we learn nothing of her marriage.

BENWICK And what if she chooses not to marry?

ANNE Oh, then the world ignores her entirely.

BENWICK The world can still see you, Miss Elliot.

ANNE You're kind, but every day makes that less true.

BENWICK I intended to marry. Perhaps you know my history. We would have been married now, had Felicity lived. I can't know how happy we would have been if we had married. All stories end somehow, at some time. We had a year together, and then she died. That was the end of that story. I agree that my friend Wentworth looks a little foolish, running around Lyme Regis. I agree there is more to life than marriage. But I also know that if you're lucky, for a little while perhaps, that other person is able to change everything. Love can save your life.

ANNE   Love can save your life? But love is the problem. I do not want to want anymore. I was in love, Captain Benwick, truly I was. Not for long, not happily for long. Everything was immediate and bright and true. And the desire, the ache for what I had then, crushes me. All I am is want. I wish I had never allowed myself to fall into that trap. But I did, and I'm still there. I can't live because I'm still there, in the past. Love ruined me. Love is a curse. I would give anything to be rid of it.

BENWICK   Miss Elliot. I do not know the circumstances of your life. I don't know what I can offer you as consolation. But I did read once that "Life has some risks. Love is one".

21

LOUISA, WENTWORTH, MARY, CHARLES *and* **HENRIETTA** *return.*

LOUISA Come on Frederick!

MARY You're getting sand on the towel.

CHARLES How else am I supposed to do it?

HENRIETTA Mary, Anne – can you help me.

ANNE What is it, Henrietta?

HENRIETTA Hold the towel over me.

ANNE *and* **MARY** *hold a towel either side of* **HENRIETTA.**

It's a shame Edmund wasn't able to join us. He's so busy with his studies.

People think that it's easy to be a vicar, but how would they like to remember all the names of the saints and so on. Other men don't need to know nearly so much.

ANNE I'm sure.

HENRIETTA And there's a huge level of responsibility. He will be responsible for the spiritual life of a whole community. I don't see how anyone can think it's any less impressive than I don't know, being at sea. Captain Wentworth has helped secure the peace, of course, but Edmund has to know the peace that passes all understanding. It's a scandal that he won't be paid more for it.

HENRIETTA *emerges from the towels in her swimsuit.*

Anne, you must come in the sea.

LOUISA I'm sure Anne would rather stay on shore. She has many books to discuss with Captain Benwick.

ANNE Captain Benwick is a very interesting young man. I'm glad to make his acquaintance.

WENTWORTH It's very good for Benwick to have some intelligent company.

LOUISA Some intelligent female company, you should say.

HENRIETTA Louisa! Captain Benwick is in deep mourning for his beloved.

LOUISA I say nothing of his beloved. All I'm saying is that he seems very keen on Anne.

ANNE How can you know that? Very keen? You take a conversation of ten minutes as proof of love? You're all mad. You have been driven mad by love.

They look at her, but it's as if they can't hear her.
MR ELLIOT *enters, crosses to* **ANNE,** *stares into her eyes and exits.*

WENTWORTH Who is that gentleman?

LOUISA Anne, do you know him?

ANNE I've never seen him before.

LOUISA But he looked at you so intently.

HENRIETTA How he admired you.

ANNE Don't be ridiculous, Henrietta.

MARY Anne, that was our cousin.

ANNE What do mean, Mary?

MARY I am sure of it. That gentleman. That was Mr Elliot. Father's heir presumptive.

ANNE I never met him.

MARY I did. When he was courting Elizabeth.

ANNE You would not remember him after such a long time, Mary.

MARY I think I may be relied on to know my own cousin. We should introduce ourselves.

ANNE Father and he parted very badly. He is Father's heir, but not his friend.

MARY This is an opportunity to repair their friendship.

MARY *tries to find* MR ELLIOT.

HENRIETTA Mary is quite right. He looked to be half in love with Anne already. He would forgive your father anything, for your sake.

ANNE I am thinking more of what my father must forgive him. He gave up our family quite suddenly. He hurt my father, and Elizabeth.

HENRIETTA We will see him make amends before long, then. His look to you was extraordinary. We will have three weddings this year. I will marry Edmund. Then Louisa will marry Frederick. You will be married soon: already in Lyme you have found two gentleman who admire you inordinately.

ANNE Have Louisa and Captain Wentworth reached an understanding?

HENRIETTA She hasn't told me anything. There's nothing to prevent their marriage: our parents are quite delighted with Captain Wentworth.

ANNE But does he love her?

LOUISA *starts jumping into* WENTWORTH's *arms, each time jumping from a greater height.*

LOUISA Catch me Captain Wentworth!

WENTWORTH Louisa!

She jumps, he catches her.

HENRIETTA They will be married in a twelvemonth.

LOUISA Catch me!

WENTWORTH Don't go any higher.

She jumps, he catches her.

HENRIETTA Nothing can stop her now.

ANNE Louisa, be careful!

WENTWORTH That's too high!

LOUISA I am determined!

WENTWORTH Louisa!

> **LOUISA** *jumps,* **WENTWORTH** *can't catch her, she falls to the ground.*

HENRIETTA She is dead! She is dead!

ANNE She is not dead.

WENTWORTH What ought we to do? Anne, what do we do?

ANNE We need a doctor.

WENTWORTH Yes. A doctor.

ANNE I'll go and find one.

WENTWORTH No. I need you here. Send Charles.

ANNE Charles, go and find a doctor.

CHARLES Of course. Yes. Right. Poor Louisa.

WENTWORTH What should we do? Anne, what can we do next? Shall we take her to the inn?

ANNE No, we should take her to Captain Benwick's house. She can rest there for weeks if she needs to.

WENTWORTH That's a very good idea.

ANNE Someone needs to go back to Uppercross and tell her parents what's happened.

WENTWORTH I'll go. This dreadful thing was all my doing. It should fall on me to tell Mr and Mrs Musgrove what has happened.

ANNE She will recover. I am sure she will live.

WENTWORTH If I go, you must stay here. They'll need you here. I'll be back in the morning.

CHARLES *returns.*

CHARLES The surgeon is on his way. He will be here soon.

WENTWORTH Musgrove, I will ride to Uppercross and inform your parents of the event. Henrietta and Mary will follow in the carriage. You stay here with Anne.

CHARLES Very good, Wentworth.

MARY I want to stay here, I want to stay with Charles.

ANNE Mary, you are quite incapable. It is better for you to be at home.

MARY I need to be with my husband. Who will be with him here?

WENTWORTH Anne will stay here. No one so capable as Anne.

MARY Louisa is my sister-in-law, not Anne's. Let Henrietta and Anne go back to Uppercross. Charles, I'm not leaving.

CHARLES Very good, Mary.

WENTWORTH But Mary –

ANNE Frederick, it's fine. We can find Louisa a room at the lodging house where Captain Benwick is living. She can sleep. She can rest. Nothing will go wrong.

WENTWORTH Anne, are you sure?

ANNE Take Louisa to Benwick's house.

WENTWORTH I'll carry her myself. How will the doctor know where to find us?

ANNE I'll stay here. I'll tell the doctor where to find you.

WENTWORTH *carries off* **LOUISA,** *followed by* **CHARLES, MARY** *and* **HENRIETTA.**

PART FOUR: BATH

22

LADY RUSSELL This fashion has not yet reached Bath. Young ladies do not throw themselves from cliffs in order to impress their admirers.

ANNE Louisa's intention was that the gentleman would catch her.

LADY RUSSELL It was somewhat ungentlemanly that he let her fall.

ANNE It was an accident. Louisa's injuries do not threaten her life and in a month or two she will have recovered. The gentleman in question is with her in Lyme. They can resume their courtship as soon as she is well.

LADY RUSELL What was the gentleman's name?

ANNE His name?

LADY RUSSELL Yes, into whose arms did she attempt to leap?

ANNE Oh. His name is Captain Wentworth.

LADY RUSSELL Captain Wentworth who you knew in...

ANNE Yes. The same man. His sister is the wife of Admiral Croft, my father's tenant. He stayed with them at Kellynch Hall. He and Louisa grew very fond of each other.

LADY RUSSELL Captain Wentworth is in love with Louisa?

ANNE Yes. I believe he is.

LADY RUSSELL This shows you were quite right about him, Anne. To think that a man who seemed to know something of your value aged twenty-three could then be charmed by Louisa Musgrove eight years later.

ANNE Louisa is a very sweet and kind girl. I hope they will be happy if they choose to marry.

LADY RUSSELL As do I. Why haven't you mentioned Captain Benwick?

ANNE Why should I mention Captain Benwick?

LADY RUSSELL Mary wrote to me that you and this Benwick had struck up a marvellous friendship in Lyme.

ANNE I spoke with Captain Benwick on one occasion, mainly about books.

LADY RUSSELL Yes and Mary tells me that the captain has bought every book you mentioned and is making a constant study of them.

ANNE I did find Captain Benwick to be a lively and clever man.

LADY RUSSELL Your sister says quite the opposite. She finds him dull and disagreeable, taken up as he is with reading.

ANNE You will have to judge for yourself. When I said goodbye to him in Lyme, he said he hoped to come to Bath.

LADY RUSSELL No doubt Captain Benwick has a long-held desire to visit the town, and your presence here is entirely coincidental.

ANNE Entirely coincidental, I am sure.

23

Enter ELIZABETH, SIR WALTER *and* MRS CLAY.

ELIZABETH Welcome to Bath Anne – we are so happy here.

SIR WALTER Tonight we will attend one of the smartest parties of the season.

MRS CLAY Lady Dalrymple's ball.

ANNE Who is Lady Dalrymple?

ELIZABETH The Dowager Viscountess Dalrymple.

SIR WALTER She is fifty-fourth in line to the throne.

ELIZABETH We have become her most intimate friends.

MRS CLAY Lady Dalrymple's ball always has the most beautiful music and dancing.

SIR WALTER I hope you can join us, Lady Russell.

LADY RUSSELL I will be there.

SIR WALTER You're looking far better than when we last saw you, Anne. Lady Dalrymple will be delighted to see such a beautiful addition to our set. What are you using?

ANNE I beg your pardon, Father?

SIR WALTER What are you using? On your face?

ANNE I'm not using anything.

SIR WALTER Just Gowland's lotion, I suppose.

ANNE Really, nothing at all.

SIR WALTER Gowland's has done wonders for Mrs Clay. You will notice she has become positively radiant.

MRS CLAY Sir Walter, you mustn't!

SIR WALTER Elizabeth's beauty is the talk of Bath. When Mr Elliot claims her as his bride, there will be many disappointed suitors cheered by the sight of Anne.

ELIZABETH Father, you talk as if you know the secrets of Mr Elliot's heart!

SIR WALTER Mr Elliot's heart is not so hard to read.

ELIZABETH Father!

ANNE Our cousin Mr Elliot?

ELIZABETH Our second cousin Mr Elliot. He delights us with his company.

LADY RUSSELL But I thought your relations with him had ended badly?

SIR WALTER It was entirely a misunderstanding. He has explained everything.

ELIZABETH Poor sweet gentleman – he thought that we had dropped him.

ANNE And have you seen much of him in Bath?

ELIZABETH We see him nearly every day.

Enter **MR ELLIOT**.

MR ELLIOT What a relief to see you at last. I have been in torment all day, wishing to make sure that Miss Elliot did not take cold yesterday.

ELIZABETH Mr Elliot is very generous in his attentions. I am extremely well.

MR ELLIOT The bloom of your cheeks is testament to that, Miss Elliot.

SIR WALTER Mr Elliot, are you acquainted with Lady Russell? Her house is very near to Kellynch Hall.

MR ELLIOT We are not acquainted, but naturally I know Lady Russell by reputation. I am honoured to make your acquaintance.

LADY RUSSELL As am I, Mr Elliot.

MR ELLIOT I have so many friends now in Somerset, that I am even more impatient than ever to visit that county.

SIR WALTER It is quite absurd that as heir presumptive you have never set eyes on Kellynch Hall.

MR ELLIOT I have read much of the beauties of Kellynch Hall and its surroundings. I always feared that were I to see it, it would be love at first sight.

LADY RUSSELL That would not be such a bad state in which to find yourself, given it may be yours in due course.

MR ELLIOT I may be heir presumptive, but I hope time will never prove me heir presumptuous. Sir Walter is still a young man.

LADY RUSSELL And if you never saw it, you could be at peace with never having it.

MR ELLIOT You are very subtle, Lady Russell.

SIR WALTER Time will show how all this will fade.

ELIZABETH And in the meantime we would take much pleasure from hosting you at Kellynch.

SIR WALTER Mr Elliot, allow me to introduce my daughter, Anne Elliot.

MR ELLIOT This lady is your daughter?

ANNE How do you do, Mr Elliot.

MR ELLIOT You will have no recollection of it, Miss Elliot, but this is not in fact our first meeting.

SIR WALTER How can that be?

MR ELLIOT If I am not mistaken, Miss Elliot, you were recently at Lyme Regis.

ANNE I was.

MR ELLIOT I was certain of it as soon as I saw you. Sir Walter, your daughter made a great impression on me when I saw her in Lyme, even though we did not speak.

ELIZABETH How extraordinary.

SIR WALTER Quite a coincidence.

LADY RUSSELL You ought to have introduced yourself, Anne.

MR ELLIOT No, Lady Russell, the fault is mine alone. I should have asked who you were. I was quite alone at Lyme. I longed to be with such a charming set.

ANNE It would have been a pleasure to have you join our party, Mr Elliot.

MR ELLIOT It will serve to cure me of an absurd practice of never asking questions. As a young man I thought it impolite to be curious.

SIR WALTER And have you now altered your notions, Mr Elliot?

MR ELLIOT They were the absurd principles of a man of one and twenty. No principle would now restrain me from enquiring about the Elliots of Kellynch Hall.

24

Enter **LADY RUSSELL**. *The other four stay on stage as*
ANNE *and* **LADY RUSSELL** *discuss them.*

LADY RUSSELL Well he's certainly not a monster.

ANNE He's charming. I cannot understand it. The last we heard
of Mr Elliot he was insulting my father all over London,
and complaining that no inheritance was worth having to
tolerate such connections.

LADY RUSSELL This is the evil of rumour.

ANNE Of course, but I know for a fact that Mr Elliot cut off my
father and sister. He seemed to be pursuing Elizabeth, and
then never visited Kellynch, never replied to their letters.

LADY RUSSELL And married his late wife.

ANNE Yes.

LADY RUSSELL It may have been her influence that prompted
his coldness.

ANNE Can it be that he did love Elizabeth, but for some reason
felt unable to marry her? His marriage was not a happy one.

LADY RUSSELL And now he is free to make a better match.

ANNE I hope so. Elizabeth appears ready to entertain the
idea. The only thing that would make me more content
than Mr Elliot being in love with Elizabeth would be proof
that my father is not in love with Mrs Clay. I fear he will
embarrass himself.

LADY RUSSELL And when you have finished marrying off your
father and sister, I hope you will tell me when to expect
Captain Benwick.

ANNE I must have misunderstood him. I'd thought he might
arrive in time for the ball, but I've heard nothing from him.

LADY RUSSELL Captain Benwick may lose his chance: there is
much to distract your attention in Bath.

25

The ball begins to get going. MRS CLAY *and* SIR WALTER
are dancing together. ELIZABETH *and* LADY RUSSELL
dance. MR ELLIOT *and* ANNE *are not dancing.*

MR ELLIOT You have had the pleasure now of meeting Lady
Dalrymple.

ANNE I have met her.

MR ELLIOT You did not find it a pleasure?

ANNE If you find pleasure in a conversational style apparently
designed to cure insomnia, then yes. Lady Dalrymple has
exactly three amusing anecdotes about minor members of
the royal family. I have heard each one twice this evening.

MR ELLIOT Don't forget she provides an occasional political
opinion that will jolt you awake with its crassness.

ANNE I am ashamed of how my father and sister fawn over her.
Ever since I arrived in Bath, I have heard nothing but Lady
Dalrymple. Even if she was very agreeable, I would regret
the fuss she has provoked, but now I find she is nothing.

MR ELLIOT One would hope for a little more refinement, but
she is an acquaintance worth having.

ANNE For what reason? Nothing in her manner, accomplishment
or understanding recommends her.

MR ELLIOT Yes, but she has value, both as good company, and
as someone who collects good company around her.

ANNE Oh, you call that good company? My idea of good company
is the company of clever, well-informed people who have a
great deal of conversation.

MR ELLIOT You are mistaken. That is not good company, that is
the best. Good company depends on birth and good manners,
and Lady Dalrymple is of such good birth that any defect
in manners can be forgiven. Rank is rank.

ANNE So you would advise me to embrace Lady Dalrymple's society?

MR ELLIOT Have you ever had your future told, Miss Elliot?

ANNE No, I have not. How do you mean?

MR ELLIOT Don't worry I am no necromancer. My knowledge of the future is very narrow – I do not even know which Anne Elliot you will become.

ANNE How many Anne Elliots can there be?

MR ELLIOT At least two. One is scrupulous, sincere, only keeping company with those who meet her very exacting standards.

ANNE And there is another Anne Elliot.

MR ELLIOT Yes, a woman who allows the world to know her. Who accepts the invitations of those who do not deserve her, knowing that it will lead in time to the company of others who are her equal. And when the world knows Anne Elliot, when it knows her gifts in conversation and her charms, I will applaud her scrupulousness in choosing a husband who is her equal. But an evening at Lady Dalrymple's is not a compromise that will harm one of Anne Elliot's character.

ANNE You flatter me, Mr Elliot.

MR ELLIOT I merely tell your future.

ANNE You think me overscrupulous.

MR ELLIOT I do.

ANNE A scruple is like a little stone in your shoe, Mr Elliot. That's what scruple means in Latin – a sharp little pebble. If I forgot my scruples, and danced on into the society of Bath, I might find when I take off my shoes that my feet are cut to shreds.

26

LADY RUSSELL Mr Elliot pays you a great deal of attention Anne. He is generally regarded as one of the most charming and elegant men in Bath.

ANNE He is very intelligent, but I find him not entirely open. I feel that he is hiding a great part of himself, and that troubles me.

LADY RUSSELL He is only reserved in a manner that is quite proper for a gentleman. You will get to know him better with time.

ANNE I will be interested to hear Captain Benwick's estimation of Mr Elliot. Captain Benwick values a straightforwardness in conversation that makes you feel his very heart is open to you.

LADY RUSSELL It sounds almost distasteful.

ANNE I don't think you will find it so. His character is so earnest that his directness never oversteps the bounds of propriety.

LADY RUSSELL Well, I am still eager to meet the captain. When do you think he will arrive?

ANNE I expect him at any moment.

LADY RUSSELL It certainly sounds as if his openness of heart appeals to your own.

27

MRS CLAY It will be a pleasure for Sir Walter to have all three of his daughters around him.

ELIZABETH Our new home can barely accommodate it. Where will Mary and Charles sleep? Surely Mary realises that we do not have the space that we had at Kellynch.

MRS CLAY Has Mary had the courtesy to ask if she can stay, or does she presume her welcome here?

ELIZABETH She says they are coming to Bath, no doubt she expects me to extend her an invitation. My God, do you think the children are coming too? There is no possibility of them staying at Camden Place.

MRS CLAY Perhaps it would be better if I return home, so that you are able to welcome them here. You will be very well looked after when both your sisters are with you.

ELIZABETH There is no question of you leaving me, Penelope. It would be intolerable to have Mary replace you. I will send her the details of some of the hotels in Bath: imagine Mr Elliot finding our house overrun with children. It is impossible to maintain a house with children present.

ANNE Does Mary send any news from Uppercross?

ELIZABETH As usual she is not well, and as usual Charles is disagreeable. Oh and Charles's sister has married, quite suddenly.

ANNE Henrietta?

ELIZABETH No, isn't she the one who is engaged to the vicar? What's the name of the prettier one?

MRS CLAY I thought Henrietta was the pretty one.

ELIZABETH No, she's not. There's one who is far prettier.

ANNE Louisa is generally considered the prettier one.

ELIZABETH Yes, Louisa has had a whirlwind romance with a naval captain and now they are married. Anne, did you know anything of this?

ANNE I knew its beginning, but I can hardly believe it has reached so quick a conclusion. You're certain that they are already married?

ELIZABETH Mary attended the wedding herself, although she writes that she finds their haste indecent.

MRS CLAY They will have wanted to settle it all before he returned to sea.

ELIZABETH Remind me, what was the captain's name?

ANNE Wentworth.

ELIZABETH Of course, Captain Wentworth.

28

LADY RUSSELL Have you heard anything else from Captain Benwick?

ANNE I must have been mistaken when I said that he intended to visit me. Either that, or his intentions have changed.

LADY RUSSELL No matter, you have the company of Mr Elliot to divert you.

ANNE He is here almost every day to visit Elizabeth.

LADY RUSSELL Anne, are you certain that his attentions are directed at Elizabeth?

ANNE What do you mean?

LADY RUSSELL Anne, I am no match-maker, I know how uncertain human calculations prove to be. All I will say is that if in the future Mr Elliot happened to ask you to marry him, and if you happened to accept his proposal, I think there is every possibility of you being happy together.

ANNE Mr Elliot is a very agreeable man, but we are not suited to each other.

LADY RUSSELL You have said yourself that you do not yet know him well. You have the rest of the season to become more suited to each other, but I will say no more. I just wonder that there is no appeal in the thought of becoming Lady Elliot. You would become the mistress of Kellynch Hall.

ANNE Mr Elliot is rational, discreet and polished, but he is not open.

LADY RUSSELL You may know him better in time. To have you near me at Kellynch Hall, and able to call it your home forever would give me more pleasure than is often felt at my time of life.

ANNE Lady Russell, I cannot love Mr Elliot. Would you have me marry him for his inheritance?

LADY RUSSELL I would have you married, Anne. Yes there is love, but there is much else in the world beside love. And love itself is a dark and shifting creature – you can never see all of it in one moment. It is far more than passion, far greater than the joy it first provokes. Mr Elliot will be the third man to offer himself to you, Anne. Will you wait for the fourth? The fifth? Of course, it is your decision. But you should make it very carefully.

LADY RUSSELL *leaves* **ANNE.**

29

MR ELLIOT Anne you sit apart, talking with Lady Russell. If I did not know how wise and good natured your friend is, I might suspect you of gossip.

ANNE I thought you told me to embrace the ways of Bath. I had understood that gossip was a central pillar of the Bath constitution.

MR ELLIOT Gossip is crucial as a pastime to occupy a great range of very ordinary people. However, you and Lady Russell are far from ordinary.

ANNE You leave me in a bind, Mr Elliot. Either I am aloof from the habits of Bath or by indulging them I become ordinary. Are there any occupations you would see me indulge?

MR ELLIOT Many of the gossips of Bath speculate on why Miss Anne Elliot does not dance. They wonder that such an elegant creature denies them the pleasure of seeing her move.

ANNE If I know anything at all about Bath, it is that a lady cannot dance unless she is first invited by a man.

MR ELLIOT This was all that was stopping you? If only I had known. Would you give me this dance, Miss Anne?

ANNE With pleasure Mr Elliot.

> **ANNE** *dances with* **ELLIOT**. *They make out.* **WENTWORTH** *appears.*

30

WENTWORTH How do you do, Miss Elliot?

ANNE Good evening, Captain Wentworth, I didn't know that you were in Bath.

WENTWORTH I just arrived. You have been here some time, I think.

ANNE Since the beginning of March. I imagine that you are only here for a short visit.

WENTWORTH I have no firm plans.

ANNE I only heard recently of your happy news. I must offer you congratulations.

WENTWORTH Oh. Thank you. What happy news?

ANNE I mean, regarding Miss Louisa Musgrove, as she once was.

WENTWORTH Oh, of course. It was a very happy day.

ANNE I am only surprised to see you in Bath so soon afterwards. When exactly was the wedding?

WENTWORTH It was yesterday.

ANNE And Louisa is not in Bath?

WENTWORTH No. She and Captain Benwick are holidaying at Weymouth.

ANNE Captain Benwick?

WENTWORTH Yes, her husband Captain Benwick.

ANNE Of course. Her husband. Captain Benwick.

WENTWORTH Yes.

ANNE I see.

WENTWORTH After their wedding, I decided to join my sister and the admiral here in Bath.

ANNE How long have Admiral and Mrs Croft been at Bath? I'm surprised we have not seen them.

WENTWORTH Oh, perhaps three or four days. Three days. Would you like a glass of wine, Miss Elliot?

ANNE That's very kind of you Captain Wentworth, but I wouldn't want to put you to any trouble.

WENTWORTH It's no trouble, I assure you.

ANNE Mr Elliot has already gone to fetch me something.

WENTWORTH Oh. Who's Mr Elliot?

> **MR ELLIOT** *returns.*

Oh. I see. Mr Elliot.

MR ELLIOT I'm so sorry to leave you for so long, Anne. Good evening, sir.

WENTWORTH Good evening, Miss Elliot.

> **WENTWORTH** *goes.*

MR ELLIOT Anne, you must forgive me. I am called home by some business that I must attend to at once. I will return to the party within the hour.

ANNE Of course, that's no matter at all.

MR ELLIOT You are such a kind lady. I will return as soon as I can.

31

MARY Any other family would deplore such haste to marry – Louisa's parents judged it romantic.

CHARLES We were all amazed to start with, as it had seemed so clear that Benwick was in love with you.

MARY No one at all thought that, Charles, don't be ridiculous.

CHARLES Well I thought it – you saw them that day at Lyme.

MARY Only someone with no knowledge of romance could take a single conversation as proof of love. Captain Benwick was very generous to talk to Anne, but she herself knows it was nothing more than kindness.

ANNE I hope Louisa and Captain Benwick are enjoying their married life.

CHARLES Louisa is so changed you would hardly know her. There is no running or jumping about, no laughing or dancing.

MARY She sits with Benwick all day, and they read poetry to each other.

CHARLES My parents like Benwick a great deal. They might wish him a little richer. They will now have to pay for Henrietta's wedding as well.

MARY They've plenty of money for that. Louisa's wedding was so cheap anyway – it all happened so quickly that hardly anyone was invited.

CHARLES We've heard that you've found many friends in Bath, Anne.

ANNE I like the town very much.

MR ELLIOT *is having an argument with* MRS CLAY.

MARY Anne, there is our cousin Mr Elliot: I must be introduced to him properly. I admired him so in Lyme Regis.

ANNE It cannot be Mr Elliot, Mary. He just returned home to attend to something.

MARY I am certain it is the gentleman we saw on the Cobb. Why, he is talking to Mrs Clay.

ANNE Mary he only just left, you must be mistaken.

MARY You know so much of Mr Elliot's movements, Anne. But I must contradict you. It is the gentleman from Lyme Regis.

CHARLES Mary is right Anne.

ANNE You are quite right Mary. I must have misunderstood him.

MARY Won't you introduce me? Mr Elliot! MR ELLIOT!!!

But **MR ELLIOT** *and* **MRS CLAY** *have gone.*

We hear lots of talk concerning Mr Elliot, many people talk of your friendship with him.

ANNE I can't imagine these people find it a particularly fertile ground for conversation.

MARY Can you not drop us a hint, Anne. I am your sister, it is unkind to keep me so much in the dark.

ANNE A hint as to what, Mary?

MARY To your engagement to Mr Elliot? Do I have to wait for official information?

ANNE There will be no information to have. I am not going to marry Mr Elliot. I'd like to know why you imagine I am.

MARY Only because all of Bath and half of Somerset talks of nothing else. That is the sum of my information in the case.

ANNE Mr Elliot's wife has not been dead much more than half a year. He is not such a man who would now be paying his address to anyone.

CHARLES Oh, if it is only a question of waiting until he is out of mourning!

MARY Then it is all settled, and in a month we can speak of it. It will be such fun to visit you at Kellynch Hall. We can easily send our boys to holiday with you.

ANNE Mary, you're being absurd. I have no hint that Mr Elliot will ask me to marry him, and if he were to propose I would not accept him.

MARY Of course you have to say that until he asks you. I would have done the same to Charles. We ladies cannot take anything for granted until the question itself is asked, but I am glad to know that it is as settled as one could hope.

ANNE Nothing at all is settled.

MARY Of course. I understand.

32

Enter **MR ELLIOT**, **ELIZABETH** *and* **MRS CLAY**.

MR ELLIOT These musicians are rated the finest in Bath.

ELIZABETH Lady Dalrymple's genius in selection makes her ball the event of the season.

MR ELLIOT I would stop a little before genius. Lady Dalrymple's taste is nothing, but she has the sense to observe London fashions and import them here.

ELIZABETH Mr Elliot, you are wicked. You know that Lady Dalrymple is my cousin.

MR ELLIOT Forgive me, I believe you did mention it. Anne, I have returned. I could not be kept long from your presence. Will you join us? We're going into the other room.

ANNE I will stay out here for a moment, Mr Elliot. I hope to find Lady Russell.

MR ELLIOT Of course. You will find a place reserved at my side.

MR ELLIOT, **ELIZABETH** *and* **MRS CLAY** *go as* **WENTWORTH** *arrives. He tries to avoid* **ANNE**.

ANNE Captain Wentworth, I hope you are enjoying Lady Dalrymple's evening party.

WENTWORTH I am not fashionable enough for a party like this. I hope that the weather will improve tomorrow. I will be glad to get out of the town during the day. I often go walking, or riding. The countryside hereabouts is very fine.

ANNE It is beautiful. Almost as beautiful as what we found in Lyme Regis.

WENTWORTH I am sorry that your memory of Lyme must be so overshadowed by Louisa's fall.

ANNE It is not wholly overshadowed. One does not love a place less because one has suffered there. Unless one has had only suffering, nothing but suffering. That was not the case at Lyme. I think of our few days there as happy ones, even though they ended so sadly.

WENTWORTH Even that dreadful event has had a happy consequence. I do not know that Louisa and Benwick would have found each other, but for being thrown together during her recovery.

Enter **LADY RUSSELL**.

LADY RUSSELL Anne, there is some music played in the other room which I am certain you would enjoy.

ANNE Lady Russell, do you remember Captain Wentworth?

WENTWORTH Madam, it is a pleasure to renew our acquaintance.

LADY RUSSELL Indeed, Captain Wentworth, I would hardly know you. You are much changed.

WENTWORTH Eight years is a great gap of time.

LADY RUSSELL The time has been kinder to you than to me. You look very well. I am delighted to know you once more.

WENTWORTH You are very kind.

ANNE I will join you directly.

LADY RUSSELL There is no need for haste. No need whatsoever. The music will last a while yet.

Exit **LADY RUSSELL**.

ANNE We can be grateful then, even for such an accident. I mean the accident at Lyme.

WENTWORTH Without it, I cannot conceive how Louisa and Benwick could have overcome their superficial disparity in nature.

ANNE Did you find it a surprising match, Captain Wentworth?

WENTWORTH I am fond of both parties, as you know. Benwick is a clever, thoughtful man. Louisa is a delightful girl. My

only surprise was that Benwick was able to attach himself
so soon after the death of Felicity.

ANNE He appeared much affected by grief when I met him
at Lyme.

WENTWORTH His heart was pierced, wounded, almost broken.
Felicity Harville was a very superior creature, and his
attachment to her was indeed attachment. A man does not
recover from such a devotion of the heart to such a woman.
He ought not. He does not. Forgive me Miss Elliot, I'm
keeping you from your friends.

ANNE That is of no importance whatsoever. Are you enjoying
the dancing in Bath, Captain Wentworth? You must be glad
now to have had Henrietta and Louisa's tuition.

WENTWORTH They were kind to make any effort at all with
me. I am a poor dancer.

MR ELLIOT *returns.*

MR ELLIOT Anne, come along. There is a friend of Lady
Dalrymple's to whom I must introduce you.

ANNE Perhaps in a few minutes.

MR ELLIOT I'm sure this gentleman will spare you, for my sake.

WENTWORTH Of course. I must try and find my sister. Miss
Elliot.

WENTWORTH *goes.*

MR ELLIOT Anne, if you are to flourish in society, you must
be careful not to get stuck in a corner. The room is full of
ladies and gentleman who are dying to become known to
Miss Anne Elliot.

ANNE Mr Elliot, you are very kind, but I am unworthy of such
celebrity.

MR ELLIOT Not a bit. Who in Bath would not wish for the
acquaintance of the most talented lady in the town?

ANNE There are many far more interesting ladies in Bath, I assure you. Is the music this evening to your taste, Mr Elliot?

MR ELLIOT Please do not change the subject from yourself. This is modesty, inapposite modesty.

ANNE Please, Mr Elliot...

MR ELLIOT Anne Elliot is too modest to allow the world in general to be aware of half of her accomplishments, and too highly accomplished for modesty to be natural in any other woman.

ANNE Mr Elliot, you have known me such a brief time to come to such definite conclusions as to my character.

MR ELLIOT I have known Anne Elliot long enough to know what a fine dancer she is. Would you give me the pleasure of being your partner in the next dance?

ANNE Mr Elliot, I am tired, and must deny you that pleasure. I will not dance again tonight. Will you excuse me.

MR ELLIOT Perhaps this music is not to your taste.

ANNE It is not a question of music. I am tired.

MR ELLIOT In any case, let us see if a different air will revive your spirits.

ANNE Nothing will tempt me to dance this evening, I assure you Mr Elliot. Goodnight.

MR ELLIOT *goes up to the DJ booth.*

WENTWORTH Miss Elliot, I am not so familiar with the customs of Bath, but do you have a partner for the next dance?

ANNE Forgive me, Captain Wentworth, I cannot dance again this evening.

WENTWORTH Are you not well?

ANNE I'm fine, only a little tired.

WENTWORTH I would happily find you a carriage, had you had your fill of the evening.

ANNE No, I will stay to enjoy the music. And the company.

> **MR ELLIOT** *has had the music turned off and makes a*
> *public announcement.*

MR ELLIOT Ladies and gentleman. I would like to dedicate
this song to one of the most accomplished ladies in Bath.
I will not say her name, leaving only need to say that her
name has long had an interesting sound to me. Very long
has it possessed a charm over my fancy. If I dared, I would
breathe my wishes that the name might never change. This
song is for you.

WENTWORTH Forgive me, Miss Elliot, I must say goodbye.

ANNE It is still very early. Won't you stay to hear the rest of
the music?

WENTWORTH No I must return home.

ANNE Is this song not worth staying for?

WENTWORTH No, in truth madam, there is nothing here worth
staying for.

> **MR ELLIOT**'s *song for* **ANNE** *begins.* **MR ELLIOT** *has*
> *rehearsed a solo routine which he performs.*

ELIZABETH Mr Elliot you have outdone yourself.

MRS CLAY There can be no finer dancer in Bath.

MR ELLIOT Anne, are you certain that you will not dance?

ANNE I will not dance with you, Mr Elliot. Please do not ask
me again.

ELIZABETH You are kind to patronise Anne, William. You
mustn't allow your duty to spoil your enjoyment.

MR ELLIOT It is not dutifulness, I assure you Miss Elliot.

ELIZABETH Why don't you invite me to dance with you instead?

MR ELLIOT Of course, Miss Elliot. Will you give me the pleasure
of this dance?

ELIZABETH I am quite worn out, Mr Elliot. I do not know that my constitution can support another turn.

MR ELLIOT If you are quite sure.

ELIZABETH But I will grant you your desire.

ELIZABETH *and* MR ELLIOT *dance.* ANNE *runs off to find* WENTWORTH. *She finds* MRS CLAY *smoking outside.*

33

MRS CLAY Anne.

ANNE Forgive me, Mrs Clay. I am expected elsewhere.

MRS CLAY Anne, it's important. Cigarette?

ANNE Please.

MRS CLAY Anne, there is much talk of Mr Elliot forming a closer attachment to your family.

ANNE This is the gossip of Bath. Mr Elliot is a fine gentleman, but my feelings for him go no further.

MRS CLAY I am sure you are far too sensible to have been impressed by Mr Elliot. It is Elizabeth I fear for.

ANNE What is your fear?

MRS CLAY When Mr Elliot is finally convinced that you will not reward his attention, I am certain he will remove his affection to her. You can see that she is still well disposed towards him.

ANNE Do you think Elizabeth would be unhappy with Mr Elliot?

MRS CLAY Would any woman be happy with a husband whose sole interest was his material gain?

ANNE You esteem Mr Elliot very poorly, Mrs Clay.

MRS CLAY I would not make such an accusation lightly. My proof comes out of the only mouth that I would trust on such a subject: Mr Elliot's.

ANNE Mr Elliot has confessed his avarice to you?

MRS CLAY He has made such accusations that only condemn himself.

ANNE Of what does he accuse you?

MRS CLAY Only of what the whole of Bath accuses me: that I am a poor widow with an eye for an easy fortune and that I have long seen a prize in your father.

ANNE He said that to you?

MRS CLAY And promised me a thousand pounds if I leave the Elliot family alone forever. When I declined his overture he became even less graceful and alluded to means within his grasp of making my union with Sir Walter impossible. I think his plan is to put into the marriage articles when he and whichever Elliot daughter marry, that your father is not to marry me.

ANNE Mrs Clay, you astonish me.

MRS CLAY Anne you are far too clever to be astonished. You must know that many consider me a fortune hunter. Mr Elliot is almost to be applauded for his vigorous steps to prevent it. As the heir presumptive, he sees all too clearly the prospect of a son of mine, a direct heir, getting Kellynch Hall, baronetcy and all.

ANNE If you have no intention of marrying my father, why not take Mr Elliot's thousand pounds?

MRS CLAY It would be very nice to have a thousand pounds. But it would hardly be honourable to take advantage of Mr Elliot's idiocy. Besides, I would not be removed from your family for ten times that sum.

ANNE Even though you do not love my father?

MRS CLAY Even though. Love can find the most surprising object. I must confess that disapproval of Mr Elliot is not my only reason for wishing Elizabeth were sensible enough to withstand his attentions.

ELIZABETH Penelope, did you hear Mr Elliot's dedication? His wish was that my name would never change. He surely means to make me Lady Elliot!

ELIZABETH *hugs* **MRS CLAY** *in excitement.*

MRS CLAY It will be a fine match, Elizabeth.

ELIZABETH Imagine me as the true mistress of Kellynch Hall. There will be no need for economy when Sir William is the master. We will have a house in London, a far larger carriage than we ever had before, so many servants.

MRS CLAY Even Mr Elliot must live within his means.

ELIZABETH But what great means they are, this dead wife was really very rich.

MR ELLIOT *interrupts.*

MR ELLIOT May I escort the Misses Elliot back to Camden Place?

ELIZABETH We must take Mrs Clay as well, William.

MR ELLIOT Alas, I only have two spaces in the carriage. Perhaps Mrs Clay would be prepared to walk?

ANNE I will walk. Mrs Clay is welcome to my place.

MR ELLIOT It is very late for such a young lady to return home unaccompanied.

ANNE Goodnight Mr Elliot.

ANNE *really gets rid of* **MR ELLIOT.**

34

Enter ADMIRAL *and* MRS CROFT.

ANNE Admiral Croft, do you know where I may find Captain Wentworth?

ADMIRAL CROFT We are meeting him, my dear girl.

MRS CROFT We are waiting for him here.

ANNE Do you mind if I wait with you?

MRS CROFT Not a bit. Is there anything we may help you with? Can we accompany you anywhere, or do anything for you?

ADMIRAL CROFT I'm sure Frederick would forgive our absence for a moment if you are in need of any assistance.

ANNE No, there is nothing I need, admiral. Thank you though.

ADMIRAL CROFT Just say the word if anything occurs to you.

ANNE You are very kind.

MRS CROFT How do you like Bath, Anne? It suits the admiral and I very well.

ADMIRAL CROFT We are always meeting some old friend or another. But we can also get away from them all.

MRS CROFT We shut ourselves up in our lodgings, and we can be as snug as we were in the cabin of the Mallard.

ANNE I had thought Bath would not suit me, but there are so many diversions here that I find very agreeable.

MRS CROFT There are too many diversions for Frederick. He is determined to get to Southampton and find a new commission.

ANNE Is Captain Wentworth leaving Bath?

ADMIRAL CROFT His intention is to leave tonight. I will join him as far as Warminster, and then he will travel on alone by post. But he can tell you all this himself. He is here.

WENTWORTH If you are ready, admiral, I would be off at once. Good evening, Miss Elliot.

ADMIRAL CROFT As you like, Frederick, I am at your service. Anne, are you sure I cannot assist you in any matter?

ANNE I am quite well. You are leaving Bath so soon, Captain Wentworth?

WENTWORTH I find I am little suited to the town's amusements.

ANNE You have had little time to become familiar with them.

WENTWORTH I remember, Miss Elliot, that when I knew you – when I knew you before. You did not used to like evening-parties such as these.

ANNE Even now, there are many occupations I prefer. But there is some pleasure to be found in the music, and in some of the society.

WENTWORTH Time makes many changes.

ANNE No, you misunderstand, I am not so much changed.

WENTWORTH It is a long time. Eight and a half years is a long time.

ANNE I promise you Frederick: even over such a period, there are feelings that do not alter.

ADMIRAL CROFT Will you away, Frederick? I am quite happy for you to stay, but if we go Sophy would have me back sooner rather than later.

MRS CROFT We would have you stay with us longer, if it were in our power.

WENTWORTH In fact, I have a letter I must write before leaving Bath. It had quite escaped me. Will you forgive me delaying by a few minutes?

ADMIRAL CROFT Anne will keep us company I am sure, or are you promised elsewhere?

ANNE I have nowhere else in the world to go.

ADMIRAL CROFT Very good. Write your letter, Frederick. I am at your service when it is done.

WENTWORTH *writes his letter.*

What do you make of this marriage of Captain Benwick's? Sophy and I were quite surprised.

MRS CROFT Felicity Harville was a very superior creature, and Benwick lost her less than a year ago.

ANNE I am glad that Captain Benwick found an escape from his sorrows.

ADMIRAL CROFT There is some truth in that, but Felicity would not have forgotten him so soon.

ANNE That may be true.

ADMIRAL CROFT It was not in her nature. She adored Benwick.

ANNE Perhaps it would not be in the nature of any woman who truly loved.

ADMIRAL CROFT Do you make that claim for your sex?

ANNE We do not forget you as soon as you forget us.

MRS CROFT Anne is right. It is perhaps a question of circumstance more than of virtue. We cannot help ourselves. Most women live at home, and their feelings prey on them. Men have a profession or pursuits or business to take them back into the world.

ADMIRAL CROFT You cannot claim this for Benwick. He has had no occupation beyond nursing Louisa.

ANNE You are quite right.

MRS CROFT Then perhaps it is true what Anne says. It is something essential to man's nature that has helped Captain Benwick find love once more.

ADMIRAL CROFT I will not allow you to claim that it is more in man's nature than woman's to be inconstant and forget

those they love, or have loved. Frederick, have you finished
your letter?

WENTWORTH Not quite, a few lines more. I shall have done
in half a minute.

ADMIRAL CROFT There is no hurry on my side. We are in very
good anchorage here. Anne, I will only mention that I have
never opened a book in my life which had not something
to say upon woman's inconstancy in love.

ANNE Please, no examples from books.

ADMIRAL CROFT Perhaps you will say these were all written
by men.

ANNE Yes! Men have had all the advantage in telling their own
story. The pen has been in their hands.

ADMIRAL CROFT So how shall we prove anything?

MRS CROFT All any of us can know is what we have felt
ourselves. The way we love and fall out of love is more
open to misconstruction than perhaps any other matter.

ANNE For my part, I have found love to be constant, to remain
even after years of absence. We do not know Captain
Benwick's heart. I hope he has found happiness with Louisa.

MRS CROFT You are quite right. Benwick's love for Louisa is no
proof that he has forgotten Felicity. Love has many facets.
Nothing about it is simple.

ADMIRAL CROFT I have only been parted from Sophy half a
dozen times, but I have seen what a man suffers when he
takes a last look at his wife as he sails away to be parted
from her for months or for years. I would convey to you
the glow of his soul when he does see her again. I speak,
you know, only of such men as have hearts.

ANNE I must do justice to you and to the men you speak of. I
cannot think that true attachment and constancy are only
known to women. We may not divide men from women on

the grounds of affection. The love I have known has been
love forever.

ADMIRAL CROFT You are a good soul, and when I think of
Benwick, my tongue is tied.

WENTWORTH I am ready, admiral, if you are.

ADMIRAL CROFT I am yours, dear boy. Let us go.

SAMUEL *runs up to* ANNE.

SAMUEL Captain Wentworth has written you a letter.

SAMUEL *hands* ANNE *a letter. He has been holding it
from the beginning of the play.*

ANNE Thank you.

MRS CROFT This is a rare trick, to write a letter to a lady sat
across the room.

WENTWORTH I thought it might be better read when I was
not present.

ADMIRAL CROFT Well, I am certain it is better read when we
are not present. We will wait for you outside Molland's,
Frederick.

ANNE *opens the letter and reads it aloud.*

ANNE I can listen no longer in silence. I must speak to you by
such means as are within my reach. You pierce my soul. I
am half agony, half hope. Tell me not that I am too late,
that such precious feelings are gone forever. I offer myself
to you with a heart even more your own, than when you
broke it eight and a half years ago. Dare not say that man
forgets sooner than woman, that his love has an earlier
death. I have loved none but you.

WENTWORTH Anne, I have been a fool.

ANNE In writing this letter?

WENTWORTH No, in every other thing. For eight years I thought you were entirely lost to me. Perhaps now I am too late.

ANNE We can't go back to what we were. Eight and half years is a period.

WENTWORTH As soon as chance threw us back together, I ought to have done all that was in my power to win back your affection. I had convinced myself I felt nothing for you and attached myself to Louisa through angry pride alone.

ANNE You know how I feel because you feel the same. I thought for a long time that I could live without you. I thought that there were more important things than love. Lady Russell could have been right: you might have had no career, and left me in poverty with five children and you dead at sea.

WENTWORTH That's not what happened.

ANNE I'm glad it didn't.

WENTWORTH I love you.

ANNE I want you.

WENTWORTH I want you.

ANNE I love you.

I suppose they have to kiss here.

Is this the end? Is everything solved with a wedding?

WENTWORTH It's an ending. It's not the end.

ANNE Will you still want to write this to me in a week, in a year? In thirty years?

WENTWORTH I mean it now. You mean it now.

ANNE And that's all we can know. Anything could happen.

WENTWORTH There could be another war.

ANNE You could be dead by the end of the summer.

WENTWORTH And we just take the risk?

ANNE "Life has some risks. Love is one".

WENTWORTH I've been lucky before. Maybe I'll be lucky again.

ANNE I hope so. Good luck, Frederick.

WENTWORTH Good luck, Anne Elliot.

The End

THIS
IS
NOT
THE
END

Lightning Source UK Ltd.
Milton Keynes UK
UKOW05f0237200517
301620UK00001B/44/P

9 780573 114526